READY, SET, SQUASH!

A Fun Guide
to the World's
Healthiest Sport

by Sonya Sasson and Wael El Hindi

Illustrations by Elena Critelli

Ready, Set, Squash!
A Fun Guide to the World's Healthiest Sport

Copyright © 2020 by Sonya Sasson and Wael El Hindi

ISBN: 978-0-578-59397-5 (Hardcover)
ISBN: 978-0-578-71465-3 (eBook)

Library of Congress Control Number: 2019916839

Front cover photo by Peter Brown
Photos of professional squash players by Steve Line
Photos of children by Peter Brown
Illustrations of squash player and Captain Squash by Elena Critelli
Illustrations of Mr. ClockWise from 123RFT.com
Illustration of squash ball on fire from VectorStock.com
Illustration of Harrow Boys' School from Alamy.com

First printing edition 2020.

LKS Publishing
145 W 67th Street, Suite 44D
New York, NY 10023

www.ReadySetSquashBook.com

CONTENTS

FOREWORD

by Sonya Sasson

At first glance, squash may seem like a simple sport. One only requires a racquet, a ball, and a wall to play. But it's so much more than what meets the eye. Squash is a combination of coordination, fitness, angles, and footwork, intertwined in a web of complexity. If rotation is off by a single degree, the ball could be sent flying in the wrong direction. Use the incorrect footwork and the ball will always be out of reach. Wael's lessons are unique because they teach how every single step of every single shot is crucial to the final outcome. It was these small, seemingly separate lessons that united into a strategy that helped propel my game.

Ever since I started playing squash, I have recorded my thoughts in a small journal. After every lesson, match, clinic, and practice, I have returned to that journal to scribble down that day's message, whether it was a few tips for playing a certain opponent or something I had learned that day. Before long, the brand-new journal had become worn out, the pages crumpled up and the covers shabby. The empty pages had been filled up with intricate diagrams, scrawled notes, and inspiring mantras.

After we had collected quite a few of these journals, a startling interrelation began to unfold before our eyes. We began to connect the dots between the lessons and tips Wael had taught me. We began to draw links between the bullet points and sketches, and soon, it all came together.

That is what this book is: a compilation of the lessons I have learned during my squash journey. Now, we look back at those journals and are reminded of the hard work, sweat, and tears that went into every one of those sessions. We wrote this book because we wanted to bestow this treasure trove of knowledge upon ordinary kids who can pick up a racquet, as we once did, and become incredible athletes and squash players. There are no conditions, no "buts," and no excuses. This book is for the kids out there who doubt themselves when it comes to pursuing their dreams. Well, let us tell you something kids: you do have what it takes.

Because with this advice and your perseverance, Wael and I believe you have the potential to soar.

Women's Professional Squash Tournament in front of the Pyramids of Giza, Egypt

WHAT IS SQUASH?

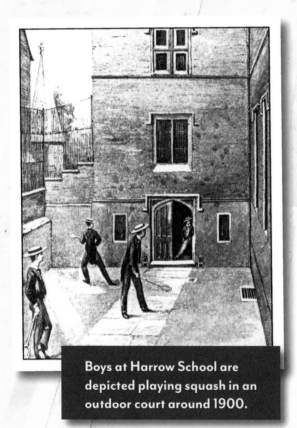

Boys at Harrow School are depicted playing squash in an outdoor court around 1900.

According to the World Squash Federation, squash has been around since 1830. The game originated from an older game called "rackets," which was played in London's prisons in the 18th century. Later, students at The Harrow School outside London discovered that a punctured ball played the same way made the game even more exciting. The first squash players used punctured rubber balls, which, when hit, squashed against the walls (hence the name "squash").

Today, squash is played in the confinement of four walls between two players, each holding a racquet to strike a rubber ball against the front wall. The sport has gained popularity around the world and is now played in over 185 countries. Some professional tournaments are held at spectacular venues such as the Pyramids of Giza (see opposite page), Grand Central Station in New York City, and the Shanghai waterfront in China!

Did you know that there was a squash court on the Titanic?[1]

THE GEAR

SQUASH GOGGLES

It is important to protect your eyes from potential stray balls and racquets.

SQUASH RACQUET

There are many different brands and weights of racquets. Try out different ones before you find the racquet that works for you!

SQUASH BALL

Squash balls come in different bounces and colors. The red and blue dot balls are much bouncier and great for beginners. Double yellow dot balls are much slower and are typically used during competitive matches and tournaments.

SQUASH SHOES

Shoes with special rubber non-marking soles are used on the squash court. Similar shoes are used in badminton and indoor volleyball. It is important not to wear these shoes off court, because you could bring dirt or liquid onto the court.

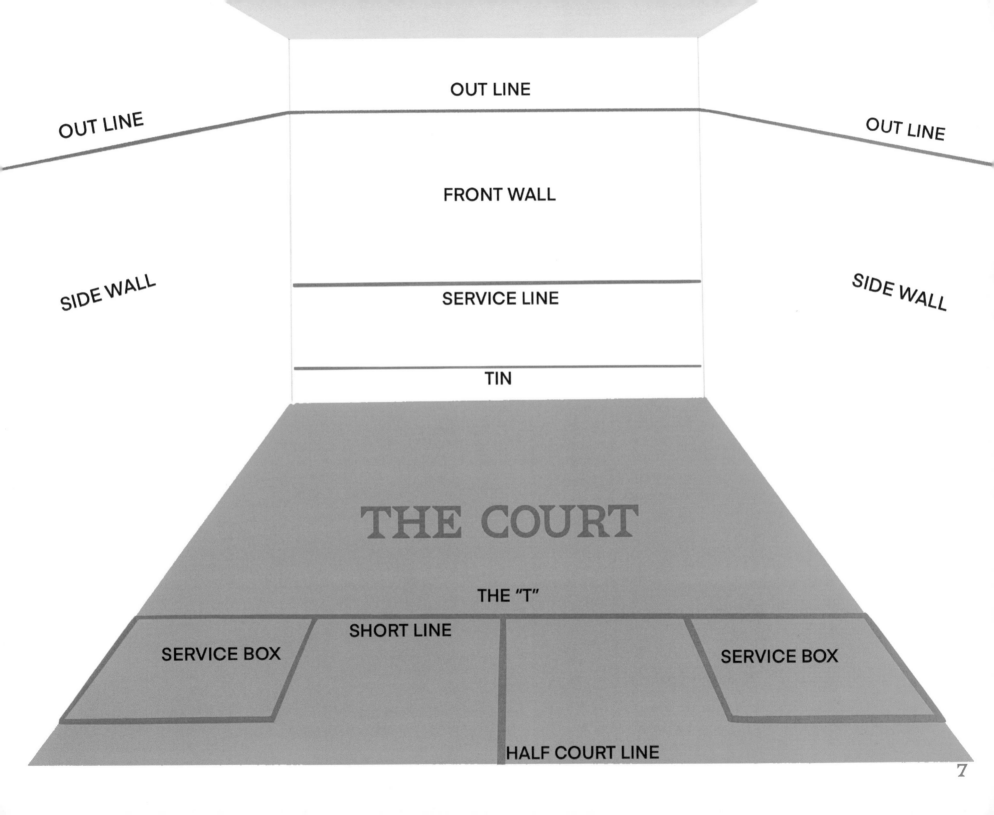

OUT LINE

OUT LINE

OUT LINE

FRONT WALL

SIDE WALL

SIDE WALL

SERVICE LINE

TIN

THE COURT

THE "T"

SHORT LINE

SERVICE BOX

SERVICE BOX

HALF COURT LINE

WHY PLAY SQUASH?

- IT'S FUN AND ADDICTIVE (in a good way!)
- Develops agility
- Sharpens hand-eye coordination
- Improves flexibility
- Increases concentration

- Builds strength
- Improves cardio health
- Increases social connections through community
- Develops self-confidence on and off court
- Crosses all age barriers
- Teaches sportsmanship

Squash was voted the healthiest sport in the world, according to Forbes Magazine.[2]

Did you know that you can burn between 500-1000 calories in just one squash match?[3]

MEET THE HEROES

Hello kids! I'm Captain Squash. Come join me on an exciting adventure to learn about my favorite sport: squash. Timing is HUGE in squash, so I invited my good friend Mr. ClockWise along to help.

MR. CLOCKWISE

CAPTAIN SQUASH

Tick-Tock kids! I'm Mr. ClockWise. I have always wanted to learn about squash – the game, not the vegetable! I can't wait to go on this journey with you.

9

WHAT ARE THE RULES?

- At the start of a match, one player spins a racquet to decide who will serve first. The winner picks which service box to serve from.

- Each rally starts with a serve, and the players then return the ball alternately (taking turns) until the rally ends. The ball must hit the front wall but can hit the side and back walls as well.

- The opponent must hit the ball before the ball bounces twice (double bounce).

- Every time you win a rally, you get a point.

- A player can also select which box to serve from at the beginning of each game and after the ball has been handed over (hand out). If the same player wins the point, they must now serve from the alternate box.

- The first player to earn 11 points wins the game.

- The first player to earn 3 games wins the match.

- If there is a tie at 10-10 in a game, players must continue until one player leads by two points.

Wait a second! So, if we are tied 10-10, how does the game end?

Whoever gets to 12 first would win the game, since 12 is 2 more points than 10.

Ohhh... that makes sense. So, if we were tied 14-14, we would just play to 16, right?

You got it!

SAFETY & SPORTSMANSHIP

1. Wear safety goggles.

2. As soon as you hit the ball, get out of the way of your shot so that your opponent can safely swing.

3. CALL YOUR LETS AND STROKES! If you feel that your opponent is blocking your path to the ball or the ball itself, don't hit the ball! Request a let or a stroke so that you and your opponent can safely continue playing.

4. Call your double bounces.

5. Respect your opponent and the referee AT ALL TIMES!

The
2 MOST
important things to
remember are to
BE SAFE
and to
HAVE FUN!

OUCH!!!

Sorry, I should've called a stroke.

COMPONENTS OF SQUASH (B.F.F.)

B — BODY POSITION

This is where you are in the court when you make contact with the ball. Create enough space between yourself and the ball to take a complete swing.

F — FOOT POSITION

Step into a shot with the foot position outlined on the clock on the next page. When you make contact with the ball, align your foot based on shot selection.

F — FOLLOW THROUGH

Swing through the ball to generate power and to make sure that the ball ends up in the correct quadrant on the front wall! Rotation is a must, and make sure to use your other hand for balance!

FOOT POSITION

FRONT WALL

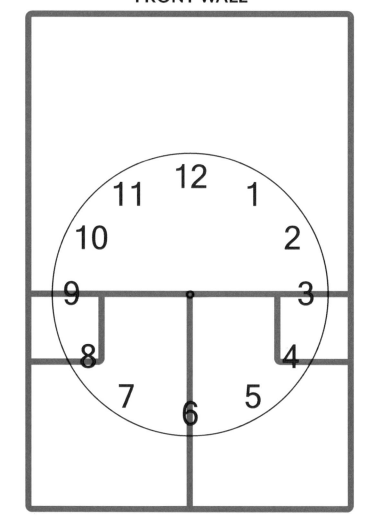

* the times for forehand and backhand are
reversed for a left-handed player

Imagine that Mr. ClockWise dropped a gigantic clock in the middle of the court. I will describe the foot position for each shot as if you are actually standing on this clock with the 12 always pointing to the front wall. This will help you remember the correct foot position for different types of shots with respect to the front wall.

WHERE SHOULD THE BALL BE HIT ON THE FRONT WALL?

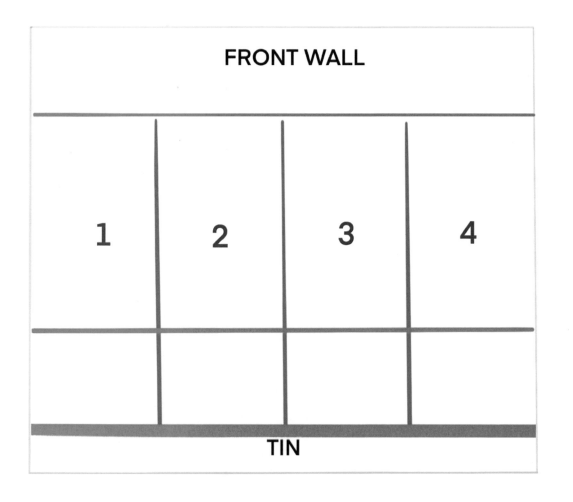

FRONT WALL

| 1 | 2 | 3 | 4 |

TIN

Imagine that the front wall is separated into 4 quadrants.

- Forehand rails are hit in **QUADRANT 4**

- Backhand rails are hit in **QUADRANT 1**

- Forehand cross courts are hit in **QUADRANT 2**

- Backhand cross courts are hit in **QUADRANT 3**

RACQUET GRIP

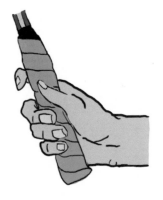

The grip is the foundation for creating the perfect swing. Here are **4 SIMPLE STEPS** to finding the **CORRECT GRIP**:

1

Hold the racquet as if you are going to shake hands with someone.

2

Create a "V" shape between the thumb and the pointer finger.

3

Split the thumb and pointer fingers away from the three "helper" fingers.

4

Curve the pointer finger around the grip.

15

Pro squash players,
Nick Matthew (l)
and Wael El Hindi (r)

16

BASIC SHOTS

- SERVE
- RAIL
- CROSS COURT
- DROP SHOT
- BOAST

Jahangir Khan spent 72 consecutive months as the men's squash world #1 compared to tennis's Roger Federer at 59 months. In fact, he won 555 matches in a row, establishing the longest winning streak in professional sports.[4]

Australia's Cameron Pilley has the fastest recorded ball speed in history at 175MPH.[5]

The serve is the most underestimated shot in the game. There are so many different types of serves. If you practice them, you can control the point from the start.

THE SERVE

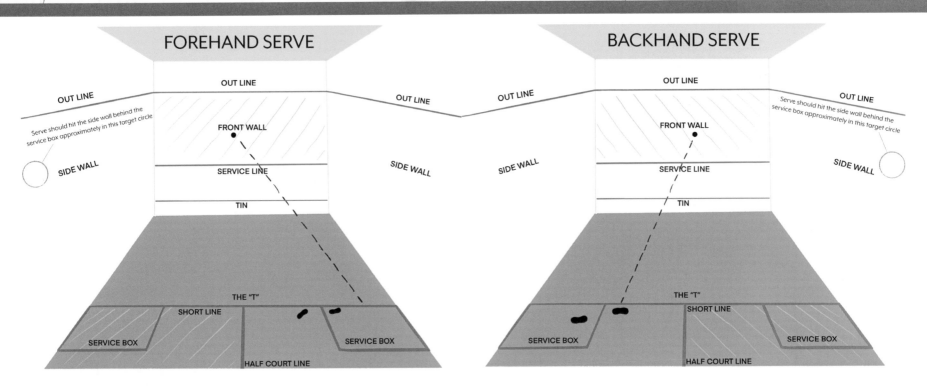

FOREHAND SERVE

OUT LINE

OUT LINE

FRONT WALL

Serve should hit the side wall behind the service box approximately in this target circle

SIDE WALL

SERVICE LINE

TIN

THE "T"

SHORT LINE

SERVICE BOX

SERVICE BOX

HALF COURT LINE

BACKHAND SERVE

OUT LINE

OUT LINE

OUT LINE

FRONT WALL

Serve should hit the side wall behind the service box approximately in this target circle

SIDE WALL

SIDE WALL

SERVICE LINE

TIN

THE "T"

SHORT LINE

SERVICE BOX

SERVICE BOX

HALF COURT LINE

FOOT FAULT

The server must have at least one foot inside the service box. If that foot is even touching the box, it will be a foot fault and the point is lost. See the diagram to the right.

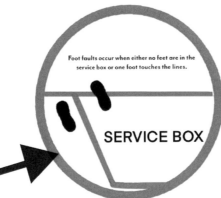

Foot faults occur when either no feet are in the service box or one foot touches the lines.

SERVICE BOX

The server tosses the ball into the air and hits it towards the front wall in the shaded region. If it hits below or on the service line, or above the out line, the serve is out and the point is lost. The ball must bounce back into the opposite quarter court. See the gray diagonally shaded area for where the ball must hit during the serve.

FOREHAND RAIL

SEE IT IN ACTION

The **RAIL** is the most basic shot where the ball has to be hit parallel and close to one of the side walls in order for it to travel to the back of the court. The rail is also known as a straight drive. The foot position for a forehand rail should be at 3 o' clock, and a backhand rail should be at 9 o' clock.

FRONT WALL

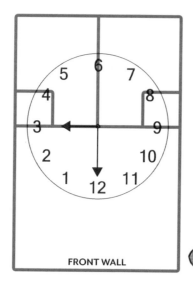

START

AT CONTACT

The ball should be in line with you and the side wall. You should be facing the side wall at this time.

CONTACT

FINISH

What if the ball bounces off the side wall and goes straight to the T instead of staying parallel to the side wall?

BACKHAND RAIL

START

CONTACT

FINISH

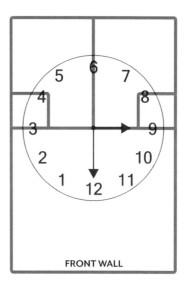

FRONT WALL

Note: The position for a **VOLLEY RAIL** is very similar to that of a regular rail. The only difference is that you are taking the ball in the air *before* it hits the ground. That's why it's called a volley!

Don't panic! Remember to check in with your "B.F.F." This is what allows you to make contact with the ball at the right time.

FOREHAND CROSS COURT

In the **CROSS COURT** shot, the ball is hit to the front wall from the right side of the court to the left side, or vice versa. The forehand cross should be hit in Quadrant 2 on the front wall while the backhand cross should be hit in Quadrant 3.

FRONT WALL

START

CONTACT

FINISH

AT CONTACT

The ball should be located slightly in front of you. This ensures that your shot will have an angle on the side wall. Make sure you stay balanced and keep your core activated during your follow through.

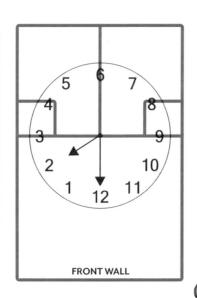

Captain Squash, my cross courts aren't getting wide enough!

22

BACKHAND CROSS COURT

START

CONTACT

FINISH

That's okay! Just remember the front wall quadrants. In order to hit a wide cross court you need to rotate your body enough in your swing and follow through to carry the ball with you. This way you can push your opponent off the T and claim it for yourself. You've got this, Mr. ClockWise!

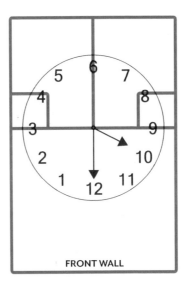

FRONT WALL

Note: The position for a **VOLLEY CROSS COURT** is very similar to that of a regular cross court. The only difference is that you are taking the ball in the air *before* it hits the ground.

FOREHAND DROP SHOT

In the **DROP SHOT**, the ball is hit softly to the front wall just above the tin so that it falls close to the front corners. Make sure the racquet stays above your wrist when you make contact with the ball. There are many advanced techniques of hitting the drop from different areas of the court.

FRONT WALL

START

CONTACT

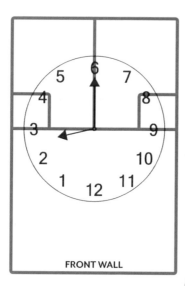

FINISH

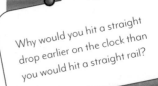

Why would you hit a straight drive earlier on the clock than you would hit a straight rail?

24

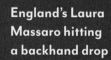

BACKHAND DROP SHOT

START

CONTACT

FINISH

You want to take the ball slightly earlier to give your opponent less time to recover.

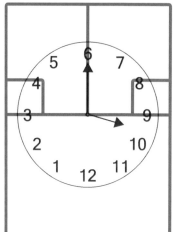

FRONT WALL

AT CONTACT

At contact, the ball should be slightly in front of you and you should make a deep lunge. The straight drop is an excellent attacking shot as it forces your opponent to run up to the front of the court to retrieve it.

25

FOREHAND BOAST

In the **BOAST**, the ball is hit to the side wall at an angle *before* it hits the front wall. There are many different types of boasts. The basic boast is used in a defensive way to dig the ball out of the back corners.

FRONT WALL

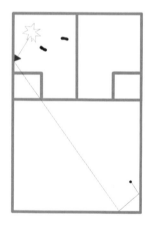

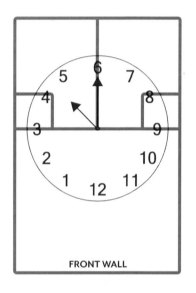

START

CONTACT

FINISH

I hit the ball after it passes me but it either doesn't get to the front wall or it hits the tin. Why?!

BACKHAND BOAST

START

CONTACT

FINISH

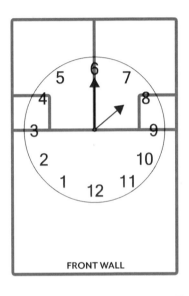

FRONT WALL

AT CONTACT

At contact, the ball should be slightly behind you. What makes this boast "defensive" is the fact that you missed the opportunity to hit a rail with the correct foot position, so you are left hitting the ball as it passes you.

Mr. ClockWise, there could be many reasons for this outcome. First, make sure you put a lot of force into your swing when you hit the ball on the side wall. Also, try hitting the ball further ahead on the side wall. With practice, you will find the proper angle.

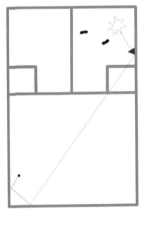

27

WINNING STRATEGIES

Move back to the
T as fast as you can
after every shot

Keep your eye
on the ball

Move your opponent
off the T (out
of position)

Hit 80% of your shots
straight (parallel
to the side wall)

Take time on your
serve and try to
hit the side wall

Focus on ONE
point at a time

Never assume your shot is a winner and always
be prepared for your opponent to retrieve it

Now that you know the rules and how to hit the basic shots, here are a few tips to help you win some points!

LET'S SEE HOW READY YOU ARE!

1 TRUE or FALSE: Squash got its name from rubber balls that "squashed" when they were hit against a concrete wall.

2 What is the minimum number of points to win a game?
      a. 6   b. 8   c. 11   d. 5

3 TRUE or FALSE: A rail is a shot hit short, usually not too high above the tin.

4 Which of the following is NOT a B.F.F. component of squash?
      a. Follow through   b. Foot position   c. Boast

5 A cross court hit from the forehand side should be hit in which quadrant on the front wall?
      a. 1   b. 2   c. 3   d. 4

Answers to the quiz are on page 31.

Malaysia's Nicol David was women's world #1 for nearly a decade![6]

WHAT YOU CAN DO TO IMPROVE

PRACTICE

Whether you're practicing alone or with your coach, repetition and discipline are how you get better! Drills are used to practice all of your skills, from serves to volleys! Another way to practice is by playing with other people. Ask some friends to get on court and play a few games with you! Remember: You only get out what you put in.

CHALLENGE YOURSELF!

See how many shots you can hit against the wall in a row!

FOOTWORK

Practice getting to the four corners and back to the T without a ball. This is called "ghosting." It will help prepare you for a match when you need to retrieve all of your opponent's shots while staying in a position to control the rally.

GLOSSARY

BACK WALL
This wall makes up the back of the court and is usually made of glass so onlookers can view the match happening inside the court. The ball can be hit off of the back wall.

BOAST
A shot hit to the near side wall before it hits the front wall.

CONDUCT WARNING
A verbal warning given by the referee to a player if they show offensive, disruptive, or intimidating behavior towards the referee or the other player.

CROSS COURT
A ball that is hit to the opposite side of the court after striking the front wall.

DROP SHOT
A short shot hit just above the tin.

FOOT FAULT
The referee makes this call if a player serves the ball and does not have at least one foot inside the service box (that foot must not touch the edges of the box).

FRONT WALL
The wall at the very front of the court. Every shot must hit the front wall to be "in".

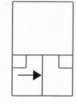

HALF COURT LINE
A line that splits the short line into two, separating the left and right side of the court.

HAND OUT
A term used when the player who is serving loses a point and the ball is handed over to the opponent who can now choose to serve from either box.

LET
The call given when a player is partially blocking their opponent's line to the ball. The point is just played over again.

NOT UP
The expression used to indicate that a shot has struck the tin or has failed to reach the front wall. The point is awarded to the opponent.

OUT OF COURT
When a ball is hit above the out line on the front, side, or back wall.

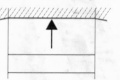

OUT LINE

The upper out of bounds line on the front, side, and back walls, above which the ball is out.

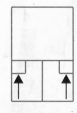

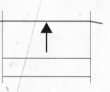

RAIL

A ball hit with good length parallel to the side wall.

RALLY

When the ball is hit continuously back and forth between the players.

REFEREE

An official who ensures that the rules of the game are observed.

SERVE

This shot begins every squash point. It is hit by tossing the ball in the air and hitting the ball on the front wall above the service line and back to the opposite quarter of the court.

SERVICE BOX

A square area marked on the court floor on either side of the "T". It defines where the server must place at least one foot while serving.

SERVICE LINE

The line on the front wall (6 feet high) above which a serve must be hit.

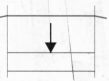

SIDE WALL

There are two side walls on a squash court.

SHORT LINE

The line that crosses the width of the court and is parallel to the front wall.

STROKE

The call given when a player is in the way of the opponent's direct swing to the ball, and the point is awarded to the opponent. If the opponent swings and hits the player, the opponent still receives the point.

THE 'T'

An area on the floor of the court where the short line intersects the half court line.

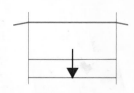

TIN

A barrier across the lower part of the front wall. All shots must make contact with the front wall above the tin to be "in".

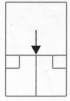

VOLLEY

A ball struck in the air before it bounces on the floor.

SQUASH RESOURCES

U.S. SQUASH
U.S. Squash is the national governing body for the sport of squash in the United States.
LINK: WWW.USSQUASH.COM

WORLD SQUASH FEDERATION
The World Squash Federation (WSF) is the global governing body for the sport of squash and helps to develop the game for players at all levels.
LINK: WWW.WORLDSQUASH.ORG

PROFESSIONAL SQUASH ASSOCIATION (PSA)
This association helps organize the men's and women's professional squash circuit worldwide. Check it out to see who's #1 in the world.
LINK: WWW.PSAWORLDTOUR.COM

SQUASH TV
Squash TV is the official live and video-on-demand website exclusively for squash developed by the PSA. You can watch live matches and replays of old matches.
LINK: WWW.PSAWORLDTOUR.COM/TV

SQUASHSKILLS
SquashSkills.com gives you access to over 4000 coaching videos from the game's best players & coaches.
LINK: WWW.SQUASHSKILLS.COM

THE PSA WORLD TOUR
Founded in 1975, the PSA World Tour organizes over 200 professional tournaments every year all over the globe!

Nouran Gohar (l) and Laura Massaro (r)

Mohammed Elshorbagy (l) and Ali Farag (r)

ABOUT THE AUTHORS

WAEL EL HINDI

Wael began squash at 13 and turned pro in 2000, reaching the podium at the World Junior Championships. In addition to dedication to developing as a squash player, Wael continued his studies and graduated the Arab Academy College with a degree in Business Administration. As a professional squash player, he was ranked in the top 10 for eight years and achieved his highest ranking at the #8 position. Now, he is focused on coaching and mentoring and brings the same dedication and talent to his job that once propelled him to success as a player.

SONYA SASSON

Sonya is a student at Stuyvesant High School in New York City. Her obsession with squash began when she was just 10 years old. She plays for Team USA's junior squad and has achieved a high rank of #6 in her division. She currently trains with Peter Nicol and was previously coached by Wael El Hindi. In her free time, she enjoys mentoring students both on and off court, playing piano, and writing.

ACKNOWLEDGEMENTS

FROM SONYA

Writing this book has been a challenging endeavor. I often found myself doubting whether I could do it. Do it on my own, that is. But I was far from alone. I had countless friends, mentors, coaches, and family help me throughout every step of this adventure. I have so many people to thank for their extraordinary contributions to this book. They have been incredibly dedicated and loyal, and I wouldn't be where I am today without them.

First and foremost, I'd like to thank my mom. You were the person who first introduced me to squash, changing my life forever. You have served as an inspiration to me ever since I was a little kid. You have pushed me to be the best version of myself in every single aspect of my life. You have constantly reminded me that I can accomplish anything if I work hard enough, believe in myself, and most importantly, stay humble and strong. I couldn't have done this without you.

Thank you to my dad and brother for always providing an innovative outlook on this project. Your fresh and exciting ideas have made this book the best it could possibly be.

Who said there couldn't have been a few laughs along the way? Thank you to Robert White, an inspiring coach and friend. You have always taught me to tackle a problem in a creative light, making me a more inventive player and person overall. I have enjoyed playing with you over the past few years, and I will never forget the laughs we have shared together.

Next, I want to thank Wael El Hindi. You have been more than a coach to me. You have been an exceptional mentor who has helped me improve my life momentously on and off court. Thanks for always reminding me to stay focused, dedicated, and confident in the work I have done.

To my incredibly awesome team at Nicol Squash—Peter Nicol, Jess Winstanley, Melissa Winstanley, Bode, Jamal Callender, Chris Sachvie, Mohamed Nabil, Olivia Fiechter, Tom De Mulder, Stuart George, and Laura Massaro—your never ending support and inspiration has helped improve my game and made me a more empowered and confident player.

Thank you to Adam Walker and Mostafa Essam for all the guidance you have given me on court.

To Timothy Arnold, Chris Walker, and Simba Muhwati: I appreciate all the insightful advice you have given me during our training.

I am so grateful to Manhattan Community Squash Center, NY Squash, and US Squash for giving juniors like myself the opportunity to play the sport we love and for working tirelessly to make squash more accessible to everyone.

And to my coaches who were with me from the very beginning: Lester, Gamal, Karim, Omar, Simone, and Stu, thank you for believing in me and teaching me the countless valuable lessons I still carry with me to this day.

FROM WAEL

I would like to thank God for giving me an opportunity to be able to do something that I am passionate about as a job, and for guiding me to help many people to unlock their potential and achieve their goals. I'm really blessed to have squash in my life.

A special thank you to my mother who made it possible for me to play squash in a condition where it was financially impossible to compete internationally as a squash player. You made it possible to overcome these obstacles and you continue to inspire me every day to help others who may face the same challenges.

Next, I would like to thank my family for understanding what I do for a living and accepting the fact that sometimes helping others can affect my time with them.

To my student and squash book partner Sonya Sasson, thank you for being a caring student in every single session and keeping a squash log. Your passion for learning and improving was exceptional at all times and you were a role model both on court and off court.

I want to thank Lata Sasson for dedicating her time and resources to this book. She made herself available at all times to make this book a reality.

I am grateful to squash associations such as US Squash, PSA World Tour and the World Squash Federation for supporting the players and growing the game. Also, thank you to urban squash programs around the world that give kids in challenging circumstances access to this amazing sport.

Thank you to FSA and HH Squash for their support.

And to everyone else, I am so grateful for everything you've done and for continuing to support my dreams.

FROM BOTH OF US

To Elena Critelli, thank you for creating all of the unbelievable artwork in this book. Thank you for making this book absolutely stunning.

To our book designers at Jera Publishing, Kimberly Martin, and Stephanie Anderson, thank you so much for bringing this book to life.

To the photographers, Peter Brown and Steve Line, thank you for capturing the true spirit of squash through your lenses.

And finally, thank YOU! We sincerely hope this book inspires you to pick up a racquet, grab a ball, and jump on court!

BIBLIOGRAPHY

1. "Squash Racquet Court." Titanic Wiki. Fandom, June 30, 2018. https://titanic.fandom.com/wiki/Squash_Racquet_Court.

2. "Ten Healthiest Sports." Forbes. Forbes Magazine, June 6, 2013. https://www.forbes.com/2003/10/01/cx_ns_1001feat.html.

3. Pitz, Taylor. "This Sport Works Your Heart at 80% of Its Maximum Rate and Burns 517 Calories in 30 Minutes." The Inertia, March 28, 2016. https://www.theinertia.com/health/this-sport-works-your-heart-at-80-of-its-maximum-rate-and-burns-517-calories-in-30-minutes/.

4. "JAHANGIR KHAN." UNSQUASHABLE, February 6, 2020. https://www.unsquashable.com/news/featured_item/jahangir-khan/.

5. Calderone, Nick. "175 Mph Squash Ball to the Back!" Right This Minute, November 10, 2016. https://www.rightthisminute.com/video/175-mph-squash-ball-back.

6. Burke, Brad. "NICOL DAVID MAKES HISTORY AS LONGEST-REIGNING WORLD NO.1 EVER." JP Morgan Tournament of Champions, December 5, 2015. https://tocsquash.com/news-posts/nicol-david-makes-history-as-longest-reigning-world-no-1-ever.

Lightning Source UK Ltd.
Milton Keynes UK
UKRC011317160920
369946UK00001B/2